Recovery from Spiritual Abuse

Juanita & Dale Ryan

6 Studies for Groups or Individuals

With Notes for Leaders

✓ *LIFE RECOVERY GUIDES*

INTERVARSITY PRESS
DOWNERS GROVE, ILLINOIS 60515

InterVarsity Press is the book-publishing division of InterVarsity Christian Fellowship, a student movement active on campus at hundreds of universities, colleges and schools of nursing in the United States of America, and a member movement of the International Fellowship of Evangelical Students. For information about local and regional activities, write Public Relations Dept., InterVarsity Christian Fellowship, 6400 Schroeder Rd., P.O. Box 7895, Madison, WI 53707-7895.

Cover illustration: Tim Nyberg

ISBN 0-8308-1159-1

Printed in the United States of America ∞

15	14	13	12	11	10	9	8	7	6	5	4	3	2	1
04	03	02	01	00	99	98	97	96	95	94	93	92		

An Invitation to Recovery

Life Recovery Guides are rooted in four basic convictions.

First, we are in need of recovery. The word *recovery* implies that something has gone wrong. Things are not as they should be. We have sinned. We have been sinned against. We are entangled, stuck, bogged down, bound and broken. We need to be healed.

Second, recovery is a commitment to change. Because of this, recovery is a demanding process and often a lengthy one. There are no quick fixes in recovery. It means facing the truth about ourselves, even when that truth is painful. It means giving up our old destructive patterns and learning new life-giving patterns. Recovery means taking responsibility for our lives. It is not easy. It is sometimes painful. And it will take time.

Third, recovery is possible. No matter how hopeless it may seem, no matter how deeply we have been wounded by life or how often we have failed, recovery is possible. Our primary basis for hope in the process of recovery is that God is able to do things which we cannot do ourselves. Recovery is possible because God has committed himself to us.

Finally, these studies are rooted in the conviction that the Bible can be a significant resource for recovery. Many people who have lived through difficult life experiences have had bits of the Bible thrown at their pain as a quick fix or a simplistic solution. As a result, many people expect the Bible to be a barrier to recovery rather than a resource. These studies are based on the belief that the

Bible is not a book of quick fixes and simplistic solutions. It is, on the contrary, a practical and helpful resource for recovery.

We were deeply moved personally by these biblical texts as we worked on this series. We are convinced that the God of the Bible can bring serenity to people whose lives have become unmanageable. If you are looking for resources to help you in your recovery, we invite you to study the Bible with an open mind and heart.

Getting the Most from Life Recovery Guides

Life Recovery Guides are designed to assist you to find out for yourself what the Bible has to say about different aspects of recovery. The texts you will study will be thought-provoking, challenging, inspiring and very personal. It will become obvious that these studies are not designed merely to convince you of the truthfulness of some idea. Rather, they are designed to allow biblical truths to renew your heart and mind.

We want to encourage realistic expectations of these discussion guides. First, they are not intended to be everything-the-Bible-says about any subject. They are not intended to be a systematic presentation of biblical theology.

Second, we want to emphasize that these guides are not intended to provide a recovery program or to be a substitute for professional counseling. If you are in a counseling relationship or are involved in a support group, we pray that these studies will enrich that resource. If you are not in a counseling relationship and your recovery involves long-term issues, we encourage you to consider seeking the assistance of a mental health professional.

What these guides are designed to do is to help you study a series of biblical texts which relate to the process of recovery. Our hope is that they will allow you to discover the Good News for people who are struggling to recover.

There are six studies in each Life Recovery Guide. This should provide you with maximum flexibility in how you use these guides.

Combining the guides in various ways will allow you to adapt them to your time schedule and to focus on the concerns most important to you or your group.

All of the studies in this series use a workbook format. Space is provided for writing answers to each question. This is ideal for personal study and allows group members to prepare in advance for the discussion. The guides also contain leader's notes with suggestions on how to lead a group discussion. The notes provide additional background information on certain questions, give helpful tips on group dynamics and suggest ways to deal with problems that may arise during the discussion. These features enable someone with little or no experience to lead an effective discussion.

Suggestions for Individual Study

1. As you begin each study, pray that God would bring healing and recovery to you through his Word.

2. After spending time in personal reflection, read and reread the passage to be studied.

3. Write your answers in the spaces provided or in a personal journal. Writing can bring clarity and deeper understanding of yourself and of the Bible. For the same reason, we suggest that you write out your prayers at the end of each study.

4. Use the leader's notes at the back of the guide to gain additional insight and information.

5. Share what you are learning with someone you trust. Recovery is empowered by experiences of community.

Suggestions for Group Study

Even if you have already done these studies individually, we strongly encourage you to find some way to do them with a group of other people as well. Although each person's recovery is different, everyone's recovery is empowered by the mutual support and encouragement that can only be found in a one-on-one or a group setting.

Several reminders may be helpful for participants in a group study:

1. Realize that trust grows over time. If opening up in a group setting is risky, realize that you do not have to share more than what feels safe to you. However, taking risks is a necessary part of recovery. So, do participate in the discussion as much as you are able.

2. Be sensitive to the other members of the group. Listen attentively when they talk. You will learn from their insights. If you can, link what you say to the comments of others so the group stays on the topic. Also, be affirming whenever you can. This will encourage some of the more hesitant members of the group to participate.

3. Be careful not to dominate the discussion. We are sometimes so eager to share what we have learned that we do not leave opportunity for others to respond. By all means participate! But allow others to do so as well.

4. Expect God to teach you through the passage being discussed and through the other members of the group. Pray that you will have a profitable time together.

5. We recommend that groups follow a few basic guidelines, and that these guidelines be read at the beginning of each discussion session. The guidelines, which you may wish to adapt to your situation, are:

 a. Anything said in the group is considered confidential and will not be discussed outside the group unless specific permission is given to do so.

 b. We will provide time for each person present to talk if he or she feels comfortable doing so.

 c. We will talk about ourselves and our own situations, avoiding conversation about other people.

 d. We will listen attentively to each other.

 e. We will be very cautious about giving advice.

 f. We will pray for each other.

If you are the discussion leader, you will find additional suggestions and helpful ideas for each study in the leader's notes. These are found at the back of the guide.

Recovering from Spiritual Abuse

It is for freedom that Christ has set us free. Stand firm, then, and do not let yourselves be burdened again by a yoke of slavery.
(Galatians 5:1)

The Christian faith is a faith designed to set us free. It was for this amazing purpose that Christ came. For many of us, however, something has gone terribly wrong. Like the people to whom Paul wrote in the Galatian church, we have come to experience the Christian life as a burden, a "yoke of slavery." The faith which was intended to lead us into a life of freedom has somehow rooted us more deeply in shame.

The Bible warns us that people who have experienced the freedom which Christ intended can still be drawn back into bondage. Faith, even faith intended for freedom, can be perverted into forms of slavery. The good news can all too easily be twisted into bad news. The gospel of grace can be transformed into the ball-and-chain of having-to-try-harder.

Many of us have experienced the deep wounds of spiritual abuse. The word *abuse* suggests that damage or injury has been done to a person. Spiritual abuse is a kind of abuse which damages the central core of who we are. It leaves us spiritually discouraged and emotionally cut off from the healing love of God.

Like any abuse, spiritual abuse can be either obvious or subtle. It comes in many forms. Parents may have appealed to God as a reinforcement of their attempts to control their children by suggesting things such as "God will be angry with you if you don't do what I say," or "God will not love you if you don't behave." Preachers may have implied that we must do more or give more in order to be recipients of God's love or blessings. Fellow Christians may have condemned and rejected us for our failures and appealed to the Bible to justify their attitudes. Rigid, dogmatic rules and authoritarian leaders may have been the norm in dysfunctional Christian institutions. These are only a few of the many forms that spiritual abuse can take.

Unfortunately, spiritual abuse is easily internalized. Even if the external sources of abuse are eliminated, we are capable of continuing to abuse ourselves. And, when we participate in self-abuse, imposing rigid and impossible expectations on ourselves, we may also find ourselves inflicting these forms of bondage on others. In this way the vicious cycle of spiritual abuse is perpetuated.

The point of these studies is not to figure out who is abusive and who is not. We do not want to encourage the pointing of accusing fingers at people and institutions that may have been abusive. None of us will ever recover by investing more energy in blame. Our hope is, rather, that Scripture will be helpful to us as we begin to break the cycle of spiritual abuse. By going back to the basic truths presented to us in the Bible, we may be able to connect again with the freedom that is our rightful inheritance in Christ.

As we will see in the texts for these studies, people and institutions become abusive when they encourage pretense and self-righteousness, when they offer a "quick fix" for life's struggles or encourage performance-based lifestyles and when they bind our spirits with the cords of judgmentalism and legalism. All of these perversions of the Christian faith lead to bondage rather than freedom. It is, however, for freedom that Christ has set us free.

Our prayer is that these studies will be a step for you in the healing of the damaging effects of spiritual abuse. May the grace of God set you free.

May your roots sink deeply into the soil of God's love.

Dale and Juanita Ryan

1
Resisting Pretense: The Struggle for Honesty

One of the first things Mike learned about the Christian faith as a young child was that "every day with Jesus is sweeter than the day before." He accepted this with the simple faith of a child. It was very confusing, therefore, when every day did not seem to be sweeter. Some days were good days, but some were bad days, some were very, very bad days. As he grew older, he found it very difficult to sustain the pretense . . . except at church.

At church he could still act and feel like "every day is sweeter." Sometimes he was angry in the car all the way to church, yelling at the kids or blaming his wife for making them late again. But as soon as he actually got to church, a remarkable transformation took place. Suddenly, he was able to smile and say, "Fine, thanks, how are you?" The week may have been miserable. He may have felt lonely or depressed or angry or afraid, but for a few hours on Sunday morning he was able to pretend that all was well.

When Mike was laid off from his job, however, it became more difficult to sustain the pretense. He would go to church, exchange social formalities, and try to focus on the victorious Christian life. Gradually, he began to experience a kind of inner panic. It was taking more and more energy to sustain the pretense, and he had less and less energy to give. Maybe, he worried, he had lost more than his job. Maybe he had lost his faith as well.

When our denial systems are reinforced by religious convictions, we experience shame and confusion. We become afraid that there is something terribly wrong with us—or with our faith. This is especially true if the religious roots of pretense can sink in the soil of existing family dysfunctions. If our family-of-origin lived by the "if you can't say something nice, don't say anything at all" rule, and our community of faith is also committed to this rule, it will be very difficult for us to learn to speak the truth. But pretense is a soul assassin. It is an emotional numbness, a soul sickness that prevents us from having access to our real thoughts and feelings. As a result, pretense isolates us from the people and the resources we need.

When religious practices or customs reinforce denial, people of biblical faith can appeal to the clear teaching of Scripture. As we will see in the text for this study, Jesus had strong feelings about pretense.

☐ Personal Reflection _____

1. Think of a specific time when you were encouraged by someone in your family or in your church to minimize the emotional pain you were feeling. What was said that encouraged you to minimize or pretend?

What did you do?

How did you feel?

2. Think of a specific time when you were encouraged to talk about yourself honestly by someone in your family or in your church. What was said that encouraged you?

What did you do?

How did you feel?

☐ Bible Study

Woe to you, teachers of the law and Pharisees, you hypocrites! You clean the outside of the cup and dish, but inside they are full of greed and self-indulgence. Blind Pharisee! First clean the inside of the cup and dish, and then the outside also will be clean.

Woe to you, teachers of the law and Pharisees, you hypocrites! You are like whitewashed tombs, which look beautiful on the outside but on the inside are full of dead men's bones and everything unclean. In the same way, on the outside you appear to people as righteous but on the inside you are full of hypocrisy and wickedness. (Matthew 23:25-28)

Therefore confess your sins to each other and pray for each other so that you may be healed. (James 5:16)

---

1. What insights did you gain from your time of personal reflection?

2. Jesus confronted the religious leaders of his day because they had replaced honesty with pretense and encouraged others to do the same. What thoughts and feelings do you have as you read Jesus' strong words?

3. Jesus uses two metaphors that contrast "inside" and "outside."

What leads us to cover up our "inside" life while working hard to look good in our "outside" life?

4. According to Jesus, pretense leads to "unclean" insides and "dead" insides. How have you experienced this in your life?

5. What effect does pretense have on our relationship with God and our experience of faith?

6. According to Jesus, pretense leads to death. According to this text from James, honesty leads to healing. What is it about honesty that leads to healing?

7. What experiences have you had with the healing that honesty can bring?

8. What fears keep us from this kind of honesty?

9. What impact does it have on you to know that God desires honesty rather than pretense?

☐ **Prayer** ⸻⸻⸻⸻⸻⸻⸻⸻⸻⸻

What do you want to say to the God who invites you to experience the healing power of honesty?

2
Resisting Self-Righteousness: The Struggle to Acknowledge Our Needs

The public exposure of the sexual escapades of another Christian leader had filled Bob with rage. "How could he do that?" he fumed. "He should be ashamed. It's a terrible testimony!"

Bob did not think of himself as self-righteous. Neither did he think of himself as contemptuous of others or full of deceit about himself. Nor had he set out to become smug and condemning. Quite to the contrary, the roots of his self-righteousness began within him as a sincere desire for moral purity. Over the years, however, he found that his desire for moral purity was gradually becoming distorted. He was losing touch with his own needs and limitations and at the same time becoming more and more angry about the needs and limitations of others.

For most of us, the driving force behind self-righteousness is a desire for protection against the awareness that we are vulnerable and needy. Focusing on the failures of other people protects us from the painful awareness of our own needs and limits. Experiences with shame have convinced many of us that it is bad to have needs. As a result, we desperately want to be strong and resourceful and are ashamed of needing help.

Religious practices and teachings which feed this shame are the soil in which religious self-righteousness grows. If God is harsh and judgmental, rejecting all but the strong and righteous, then we will find ourselves working compulsively to look strong and righteous. But if God is full of mercy, and if God does not shame us for our needs, then it may be possible for us to learn to accept our needs.

The Bible is clear about God's acceptance of our needs. God invites us to acknowledge our needs. As we do so, we experience the vulnerability that we share with all other humans. As we embrace our own human struggle, it becomes possible for us to meaningfully embrace our brothers and sisters as well.

□ Personal Reflection ─────────────────────────

1. How did the members of your family respond to your physical needs?

your spiritual needs?

your emotional needs?

2. How have you seen people in your community of faith respond to physical needs?

to spiritual needs?

to emotional needs?

3. What thoughts and feelings do you have about your own needs?

☐ **Bible Study**_____

To some who were confident of their own righteousness and looked down on everybody else, Jesus told this parable: "Two men went up to the temple to pray, one a Pharisee and the other a tax collector.

The Pharisee stood up and prayed about himself: 'God, I thank you that I am not like other men—robbers, evildoers, adulterers—or even like this tax collector. I fast twice a week and give a tenth of all I get.'

"But the tax collector stood at a distance. He would not even look up to heaven, but beat his breast and said, 'God, have mercy on me, a sinner.'

"I tell you that this man, rather than the other, went home justified before God. For everyone who exalts himself will be humbled, and he who humbles himself will be exalted." (Luke 18:10-14)

---

1. What insights did you gain from your time of personal reflection?

2. Jesus told this story for the benefit of people who "were confident of their own righteousness and looked down on everyone else." What are the dangers of this kind of self-righteousness?

3. When have you found yourself thinking and feeling like the Pharisee in this story?

What was that experience like for you?

4. The Pharisee compares himself with the tax collector and concludes that he is spiritually superior. What are the dangers of comparing ourselves with others?

5. Jesus also told this story for the benefit of people who have experienced rejection, shame and abuse from self-righteous people. What experiences have you had with people who are confident of their own righteousness and look down on others?

What impact have these experiences had on you?

6. Unlike the Pharisee, the tax collector was able to acknowledge his need. What is the advantage to being able to acknowledge our needs?

7. Many people associate the word *humble* with low self-esteem. But the solution for self-righteousness is not low self-esteem. How does humility differ from low self-esteem?

8. What effect does it have on you to know that God does not shame you for your needs but instead pronounces blessing when you have the courage to acknowledge your needs?

☐ **Prayer** _____

What do you want to say to the God who pronounces blessing on people who acknowledge their needs?

3

Resisting the Quick Fix: The Struggle to Persevere

"Just put the past behind you. Leave it at the foot of the cross. Claim the victory, and you will experience the abundant life."

Sharon's husband, the pastor of a local church, often preached this message to the congregation. And Sharon desperately wanted to be able to put this message into practice. She wanted to forget the painful memories, to be a pain-free Christian just like her husband seemed to be. But she had put the past behind her a thousand times, and the pain had not gone away. She knew that healing came from turning her cares over to God, but she had done that. Again and again. She had forgiven. And forgiven again. She had repented. And repented again. She had rebuked demonic influences, claimed the promises of God, come forward, committed her life, recommitted her life, again and again and again. She had done it all. Why, she wept, wasn't she better yet? She felt like a failure as a Christian.

Religious teachings that if only we would do some "simple" thing (trust God, pray, forget, repent) then our problems would be solved lead to increased pretense and denial and to all of the painful feelings of failure that come with pretense and denial. The pursuit of "quick fixes" leads to helplessness and despair. Fortunately, the Bible does not teach that faith in Christ will make our problems disappear. It does not teach that avoiding or pretending about our human feelings is a requirement of faithfulness. Rather, it teaches us that faith is a life-long process of transformation and that even people of great faith will struggle with human feelings and needs. It is when we embrace our human feelings as part of the journey of faith that our faith takes on new depth and richness.

Recovery from spiritual abuse will require many of us to face the truth about quick fixes and to abandon these in favor of the long and difficult journey of recovery.

☐ **Personal Reflection** _____

1. How do you feel about yourself when you can't seem to "hurry up and feel better"?

2. What sorts of things have people said to you that have reinforced the idea that because you are a Christian you "ought" to feel better by now?

3. What would help you to stay committed to the process of healing and growing rather than seeking another quick fix?

☐ **Bible Study**_____

I cried out to God for help;
  I cried out to God to hear me.
When I was in distress, I sought the Lord;
  at night I stretched out untiring hands
  and my soul refused to be comforted.

I remembered you, O God, and I groaned;
  I mused, and my spirit grew faint.

You kept my eyes from closing;
  I was too troubled to speak.
I thought about the former days,
  the years of long ago;
I remembered my songs in the night.
  My heart mused and my spirit inquired:

"Will the Lord reject forever?
  Will he never show his favor again?
Has his unfailing love vanished forever?
  Has his promise failed for all time?
Has God forgotten to be merciful?
  Has he in anger withheld his compassion?"

Then I thought, "To this I will appeal:

the years of the right hand of the Most High."
I will remember the deeds of the LORD;
yes, I will remember your miracles of long ago.
I will meditate on all your works
and consider all your mighty deeds. (Psalm 77:1-12)

---

1. What insights did you gain from your time of personal reflection?

2. What words and phrases does the psalmist use to describe his struggle?

3. What clues does the psalmist give about how long he has been suffering?

4. What is difficult about struggles that seem to go on for a long time?

5. How does the psalmist's experience compare with your own?

6. Like all of the psalms, this psalm was probably used as a part of public worship. Apparently, the emotions that come during the long haul of recovery were thought to be important enough to be expressed as the community of faith gathered to worship. What effect would it have on you if your community of faith regularly and publicly acknowledged that we experience the kinds of emotions found in this text?

7. Although the psalmist struggles with some very painful memories, he decides to focus on memories of God's works and mighty deeds in the past. How could focusing on such memories help us persevere when healing is slow?

8. We want to be "better by now." Other people may also want us to be "better by now." How would it help you to know that God is not disappointed with the pace of your recovery but, rather, is prepared to be involved with you no matter now long your recovery takes?

☐ **Prayer** ————————————————————————————

What do you want to say to the God who understands that healing takes time?

4
Resisting Performance: The Struggle for Freedom and Grace

Joann is the head nurse on a busy medical unit at a university hospital. She works long hours with few breaks. She is also a single parent with two teenaged children. Her daughter is a straight-A student and a cheerleader, but her son is doing poorly in school and drinks with his friends on the weekends. Joann lies awake at night wondering if he will end up like her alcoholic father who spent his life either working at odd jobs or drinking.

Joann teaches Sunday school and sings in the church choir and is a member of the Christian education committee at her church. She also spends a lot of time on the phone listening to friends who call her with problems. Joann has no time to herself. She gets very little sleep. She is always working or giving of herself in some way. As a result, Joann is exhausted, depressed and angry.

Joann's struggle is familiar to many of us. We work hard. We give and give and give of ourselves. But no matter how much we do, it never seems to be enough to meet other people's expectations of us. And we worry that it will not be enough to meet God's expectations of us either.

Religious teachings and practices that reinforce our compulsive, driven, performance-based lifestyles are commonplace. It's not good enough to pray; we should pray all the time (or at least very early in the morning!). It's not good enough to read the Bible; we should read it constantly. It's not good enough to do God's will. We should strive to do God's "perfect" will. Unfortunately, no amount of religious gymnastics can turn our compulsive behavior into righteousness. We just become more and more driven, more and more out of touch with ourselves and more and more afraid. Fortunately, as we will see in the text for this study, the Bible speaks quite directly and clearly to the religious compulsivity that results in a performance-driven life.

☐ Personal Reflection _____

1. What performance expectations do you think other Christians have of you?

2. What expectations do you worry God might have of you?

3. In what ways have you found yourself performing for God or for others?

4. What do you worry might happen if you do not perform?

☐ **Bible Study**_____

With what shall I come before the LORD
   and bow down before the exalted God?
Shall I come before him with burnt offerings,
    with calves a year old?
Will the LORD be pleased with thousands of rams,
    with ten thousand rivers of oil?
Shall I offer my firstborn for my transgression,
    the fruit of my body for the sin of my soul?
He has showed you, O man, what is good.
    And what does the LORD require of you?
To act justly and to love mercy
    and to walk humbly with your God. (Micah 6:6-8)

But because of his great love for us, God, who is rich in mercy, made us alive with Christ even when we were dead in transgressions— it is by grace you have been saved. . . . For it is by grace you have been saved, through faith—and this not from yourselves, it is the gift of God—not by works, so that no one can boast. (Ephesians 2:4-5, 8-9)

1. What insights did you gain from your time of personal reflection?

2. The prophet Micah considers three possible responses to his question about how to "come before God." Each possibility involves performing increasingly extreme religious behaviors. How would you restate these possibilities in terms of religious behaviors that are more common today?

3. Religious communities which teach that spiritual well-being is contingent upon the performance of certain religious practices are very popular both within the Christian tradition and in other religious traditions. What do you think is the attraction of performance-centered religion?

4. When people get caught up in religious performances they are acting on certain assumptions about God. What assumptions about God's character cause us to feel we need to perform in order to "come before" him?

5. Micah suggests that no religious behaviors can make it possible for us to "come before" God. Rather than extremes of religious performance, Micah focuses on our relationships with each other and with God. What does it mean to "act justly and love mercy"?

What does it mean to "walk humbly with your God"?

6. Micah is contrasting a performance-centered religion with a relationship-centered faith. What does it suggest about God's character that he values relationships rather than performance?

7. The passage from Ephesians also makes the point that the Christian faith is not about religious performances. What does this text say about how we can have a relationship with God?

8. How is God described in the passage from Ephesians?

9. How does this description of God compare with your images of God?

10. How might we help each other to become less compulsive about religious performances and more focused on the relationships which are most important in life?

☐ **Prayer** ————————————————————————————

What do you want to say to the God who offers you grace and freedom?

5
Resisting Judgmentalism: The Struggle for Compassion

When Janet came to church on Sunday morning for the first time, she had been sober for almost a year. After 25 years of chronic alcohol abuse, she had come to the end of her resources and now spoke of a powerful experience of God as a higher power. It was time, she thought, to make an effort to reconnect with the faith of her childhood—she knew that her "higher power" had a name. But she did not feel comfortable at church. She didn't know how to be politically correct in the social context of the church.

It was a short conversation overheard in the church hallway that turned her hopefulness about participation in the Christian community into shame.

"I've seen her come out of that bar on the corner," the first person said.

"Really?" the other responded. "I can't understand why Pastor Dan encourages those support groups anyway. We'll never get the new building program going if the only kind of people we attract to the congregation are people like her."

All Janet could think about was "these people only know the tip of the iceberg." What would people say if they knew about the abortions, the painful series of abusive relationships? What if they knew the sordid details? The blackouts, the lies, the secrets, the betrayals? What then? Janet struggled with deep spiritual discouragement as she drove home from church that day. She could feel the shame growing in her. Maybe she really wasn't good enough to be a Christian anyway.

Judgmentalism is a powerful form of spiritual abuse and a source of spiritual discouragement. It is, unfortunately, very common. It comes to us very easily. We use it often as a weapon against ourselves and against others. Sometimes it comes wrapped in the language of lofty moral crusades, sometimes it is a simple unadorned rejection. But whenever and however it comes, it does damage to the emotional and spiritual core of our persons.

As we will see in the text for this study, the Bible warns against judgmentalism and offers us an alternative. It is the alternative of compassion.

☐ Personal Reflection _____

1. Think of a time when you felt you were being judged by someone. What was the impact of that judgment on you emotionally and spiritually?

2. Think of a time when you experienced compassionate understanding from someone. What was the impact of that experience on you?

☐ Bible Study

Do not judge, or you too will be judged. For in the same way you judge others, you will be judged, and with the measure you use, it will be measured to you.

Why do you look at the speck of sawdust in your brother's eye and pay no attention to the plank in your own eye? How can you say to your brother, "Let me take the speck out of your eye, when all the time there is a plank in your own eye? You hypocrite, first take the plank out of your own eye, and then you will see clearly to remove the speck from your brother's eye." (Matthew 7:1-5)

Brothers, if someone is caught in a sin, you who are spiritual should restore him gently. But watch yourself, or you also may be tempted. Carry each other's burdens, and in this way you will fulfill the law of Christ. (Galatians 6:1-2)

---

1. What insights did you gain from your time of personal reflection?

2. What are some possible answers to Jesus' question, "Why do you look at the speck of sawdust in your brother's eye and pay no attention to the plank in your own eye?" Why do we look at the speck in someone else's eye and ignore the plank in our own?

3. Jesus clearly teaches that we ought not to judge other people. What are the problems and dangers of judging others?

4. What assumptions do we make about ourselves when we judge another person?

about the other person?

5. What are the benefits of following Jesus' teaching?

6. Jesus' teaching on judgmentalism does not mean that we should be unresponsive when someone is "caught" in destructive behaviors. What makes the difference between judgmentalism and healthy intervention?

7. What would it mean to restore a person gently?

8. How might it help you to know that God wants us to be gentle and compassionate rather than judgmental?

9. How might we help each other to avoid judgmentalism and to become people of compassion?

☐ **Prayer** _____

What do you want to say to the God of gentleness and compassion?

6
Resisting Legalism: The Struggle for Love

"I know all the rules about being a good Christian," eight-year-old Julia told her friend. "Don't smoke. Don't drink. Don't steal. And don't complain." After a moment's hesitation she added, "I saw your daddy smoking, so I don't want to be your friend anymore."

It seems ridiculous and childish, of course. But the truth is that we adults are sometimes very much like young Julia. Clear, rigid rules seem to have an enormous appeal. The appeal can be so strong that we fail to see how they can be abusive to ourselves and to others. We prefer following rules to loving our neighbor.

One of the rewards of legalism is the control which it offers. By performing according to the rules, we can control how we feel about ourselves. Obey the rules, feel good. Disobey the rules, feel bad. In some forms of Christian legalism we can even control God. Obey the rules, God is happy. Disobey the rules, God is sad. We can control God's mood! That's a lot of control.

We impose legalistic restrictions on ourselves and on others as a way of proving our goodness to ourselves, to others and to God, all the time forgetting the rule that is most important, the rule of love.

The rule of love frightens us because we cannot measure it or quantify it or control it. It doesn't allow us to prove anything to anybody. The Bible is relentless, however, in calling us out of bondage to religious rules. It calls us to leave legalism and to follow the way of love.

☐ Personal Reflection _____

1. What rules were you taught to follow in order to demonstrate that you were a "good Christian"?

2. Which of these rules have been helpful to you and which have not been helpful?

What are the differences between the rules that have been helpful and those that have not?

3. How have these rules affected your relationships with the most important people in your life?

☐ **Bible Study**━━━━━━━━━━━━━━━━━━━━━━━━━━━━

On another Sabbath he went into the synagogue and was teaching, and a man was there whose right hand was shriveled. The Pharisees and the teachers of the law were looking for a reason to accuse Jesus, so they watched him closely to see if he would heal on the Sabbath. But Jesus knew what they were thinking and said to the man with the shriveled hand, "Get up and stand in front of everyone." So he got up and stood there.

Then Jesus said to them, "I ask you, which is lawful on the Sabbath: to do good or to do evil, to save life or to destroy it?"

He looked around at them all, and then said to the man, "Stretch out your hand." He did so, and his hand was completely restored. But they were furious and began to discuss with one another what they might do to Jesus. (Luke 6:6-11)

---

1. What insights did you gain from your time of personal reflection?

2. Resting from work on the Sabbath was a central obligation in the Jewish tradition. Many human-made rules were developed to spell out the exact meaning of Sabbath rest. In this story Jesus broke one of these religious rules. What thoughts and feelings do you have about Jesus deliberately breaking this rule?

3. Jesus could have healed this man on the following day. Why would he make a point of publicly breaking a religious rule in order to heal the man?

4. What point is Jesus making when he asks, "Which is lawful on the Sabbath: to do good or to do evil, to save life or to destroy it?"

5. What do you make of the anger the religious leaders had toward Jesus for healing this man?

6. What does this story about Jesus tell us about God?

7. In what ways has legalism been harmful to you?

8. How might the priority Jesus gives to healing over rule-keeping help you in your struggle with spiritual abuse?

☐ **Prayer** ——————————————————————

What do you want to say to the God who loves you?

Leader's Notes

You may be experiencing a variety of feelings as you anticipate leading a group using a Life Recovery Guide. You may feel inadequate and afraid of what will happen. If this is the case, know you are in good company. Many of the kings, prophets and apostles in the Bible felt inadequate and afraid. Many other small group leaders share the experience of fear as well.

Your willingness to lead, however, is a gift to the other group members. It might help if you tell them about your feelings and ask them to pray for you. Keep in mind that the other group members share the responsibility for the group. And realize that it is God's work to bring insight, comfort, healing and recovery to group members. Your role is simply to provide guidance for the discussion. The suggestions listed below will help you to provide that guidance.

Using the Life Recovery Guide Series

This Life Recovery Guide is one in a series of guides. The series was designed to be a flexible tool that can be used in various combinations by individuals and groups—such as support groups, Bible studies and Sunday-school classes. Each guide contains six studies. If eight guides are used, they can provide a year-long curriculum series. Or if the guides are used in pairs, they can provide studies for a quarter (twelve weeks).

We want to emphasize that all of the guides in this series are designed to be useful to anyone. Each guide has a specific focus, but all are written with a general audience in mind. Additionally, the workbook format allows for personal interaction with biblical truths, making the guides adaptable to each individual's unique journey in recovery.

The guides which all individuals and groups should find they can most easily relate to are *Recovery from Distorted Images of God, Recovery from Loss, Recovery from Bitterness, Recovery from Shame* and *Recovery from Fear.* All of us need to replace our distorted images of God with biblically accurate images. All of us experience losses, disappointments and disillusionment in life, as well as loss through death or illness. We all have life experiences and relationships which lead to bitterness and which make forgiveness difficult. And we all experience shame and fear and their debilitating consequences.

Other guides such as *Recovery from Codependency, Recovery from Family Dysfunctions, Recovery from Abuse, Recovery from Spiritual Abuse* and *Recovery from Addictions* have a more specific focus, but they address issues of very general concern both within the Christian community and in our culture as a whole. The biblical resources will be helpful to your recovery even if you do not share the specific concerns which these guides address.

Individuals who are working on a specific life issue and groups with a shared focus may want to begin with the guide which relates most directly to their concerns. Survivors of abuse, for example, may want to work through *Recovery from Abuse* and follow it with *Recovery from Shame.* Adult children from dysfunctional families may want to begin with *Recovery from Family Dysfunctions* and then use *Recovery from Distorted Images of God.* And those who struggle with addictive patterns may want to begin with *Recovery from Addictions* and then use *Recovery from Codependency.*

There are many other possibilities for study combinations. The short descriptions of each guide on the last page, as well as the information on the back of each guide will help you to further decide which guides will be most helpful to your recovery.

Preparing to Lead

1. Develop realistic expectations of yourself as a small group leader. Do not feel that you have to "have it all together." Rather, commit yourself to an ongoing discipline of honesty about your own needs. As you grow in honesty about your own needs, you will grow as well in your capacity for compassion, gentleness and patience with yourself and with others. As a leader, you can encourage an atmosphere of honesty by being honest about yourself.

2. Pray. Pray for yourself and your own recovery. Pray for the group members. Invite the Holy Spirit to be present as you prepare and as you meet.

3. Read the study several times.

4. Take your time to thoughtfully work through each question, writing out your answers.

5. After completing your personal study, read through the leader's notes for the study you are leading. These notes are designed to help you in several ways. First, they tell you the purpose the authors had in mind while writing the study. Take time to think through how the questions work together to accomplish that purpose. Second, the notes provide you with additional background information or comments on some of the questions. This information can be useful if people have difficulty understanding or answering a question. Third, the leader's notes can alert you to potential problems you may encounter during the study.

6. If you wish to remind yourself during the group discussion of anything mentioned in the leader's notes, make a note to yourself below that question in your study guide.

Leading the Study

1. Begin on time. You may want to open in prayer, or have a group member do so.

2. Be sure everyone has a study guide. Decide as a group if you want people to do the study on their own ahead of time. If your time together is limited, it will be helpful for people to prepare in advance.

3. At the beginning of your first time together, explain that these studies are meant to be discussions, not lectures. Encourage the members of the group to participate. However, do not put pressure on those who may be hesitant to speak during the first few sessions. Clearly state that people do not need to share anything they do not feel safe sharing. Remind people that it will take time to trust each other.

4. Read aloud the group guidelines listed in the front of the guide. These commitments are important in creating a safe place for people to talk and trust and feel.

5. The covers of the Life Recovery Guides are designed to incorporate both symbols of the past and hope for the future. During your first meeting, allow the group to describe what they see in the cover and respond to it.

6. Read aloud the introductory paragraphs at the beginning of the discussion for the day. This will orient the group to the passage being studied.

7. The personal reflection questions are designed to help group members focus on some aspect of their experience. Hopefully, they will help group members to be more aware of the frame of reference and life experience which they bring to the study. The personal reflection section can be done prior to the group meeting or as the first part of the meeting. If the group does not prepare in advance, approximately ten minutes will be needed for individuals to consider these questions.

The personal reflection questions are not designed to be used directly for group discussion. Rather, the first question in the Bible study section is intended to give group members an opportunity to reveal what they feel safe sharing from their time of personal reflection.

8. Read the passage aloud. You may choose to do this yourself, or prior to the study you might ask someone else to read.

9. As you begin to ask the questions in the guide, keep several things in mind. First, the questions are designed to be used just as they are written. If you wish, you may simply read them aloud to the group. Or you may prefer to express them in your own words. However, unnecessary rewording of the questions is not recommended.

Second, the questions are intended to guide the group toward understanding and applying the main idea of the study. You will find the purpose of each study described in the leader's notes. You should try to understand how the study questions and the biblical text work together to lead the group in that direction.

There may be times when it is appropriate to deviate from the study guide. For example, a question may have already been answered. If so, move on to the next question. Or someone may raise an important question not covered in the guide. Take time to discuss it! The important thing is to use discretion. There may be many routes you can travel to reach the goal of the study. But the easiest route is usually the one we have suggested.

10. Don't be afraid of silence. People need time to think about the question before formulating their answers.

11. Draw out a variety of responses from the group. Ask, "Who else has some thoughts about this?" or "How did some of the rest of your respond?" until several people have given answers to the question.

12. Acknowledge all contributions. Try to be affirming whenever possible. Never reject an answer. If it seems clearly wrong to you, ask, "Which part of the text led you to that conclusion?" or "What do the rest of you think?"

13. Realize that not every answer will be addressed to you, even though this will probably happen at first. As group members become more at ease, they will begin to interact more effectively with each other. This is a sign of a healthy discussion.

14. Don't be afraid of controversy. It can be very stimulating. Dif-

ferences can enrich our lives. If you don't resolve an issue complete-ly, don't be frustrated. Move on and keep it in mind for later. A subsequent study may resolve the problem. Or, the issue may not be resolved—not all questions have answers!

15. Stick to the passage under consideration. It should be the source for answering the questions. Discourage the group from unnecessary cross-referencing. Likewise, stick to the subject and avoid going off on tangents.

16. Periodically summarize what the group has said about the topic. This helps to draw together the various ideas mentioned and gives continuity to the study. But be careful not to use summary statements as an opportunity to give a sermon!

17. During the discussion, feel free to share your own responses. Your honesty about your own recovery can set a tone for the group to feel safe in sharing. Be careful not to dominate the time, but do allow time for your own needs as a group member.

18. Each study ends with a time for prayer. There are several ways to handle this time in a group. The person who leads each study could lead the group in a prayer or you could allow time for group participation. Remember that some members of your group may feel uncomfortable about participating in public prayer. It might be help-ful to discuss this with the group during your first meeting and to reach some agreement about how to proceed.

19. Realize that trust in a group grows over time. During the first couple meetings, people will be assessing how safe they will feel in the group. Do not be discouraged if people share only superficially at first. The level of trust will grow slowly but steadily.

Listening to Emotional Pain

Life Recovery Guides are designed to take seriously the pain and struggle that is part of life. People will experience a variety of emo-tions during these studies. Your role as group leader is not to act as a professional counselor. Instead it is to be a friend who listens to emotional pain. Listening is a gift you can give to hurting people. For many, it is not an easy gift to give. The following suggestions can help you listen more effectively to people in emotional pain.

1. Remember that you are not responsible to take the pain away. People in helping relationships often feel that they are being asked to make the other person feel better. This is usually related to the helper's own patterns of not being comfortable with painful feelings.

2. Not only are you not responsible to take the pain away, one of the things people need most is an opportunity to face and to experience the pain in their lives. They have usually spent years denying their pain and running from it. Healing can come when we are able to face our pain in the presence of someone who cares about us. Rather than trying to take the pain away, commit yourself to listening attentively as it is expressed.

3. Realize that some group members may not feel comfortable with expressions of sadness or anger. You may want to acknowledge that such emotions are uncomfortable, but remind the group that part of recovery is to learn to feel and to allow others to feel.

4. Be very cautious about giving answers and advice. Advice and answers may make you feel better or feel competent, but they may also minimize peoples' problems and their painful feelings. Simple solutions rarely work, and they can easily communicate "You should be better now" or "You shouldn't really be talking about this."

5. Be sure to communicate direct affirmation any time people talk about their painful emotions. It takes courage to talk about our pain because it creates anxiety for us. It is a great gift to be trusted by those who are struggling.

The following notes refer to the questions in the Bible study portion of each study:

Study 1. Resisting Pretense: The Struggle for Honesty. Matthew 23:25-28; James 5:16.

Purpose: To encourage the struggle for honesty.

Question 2. Some people will be relieved that Jesus comes down so strongly on the side of honesty and of paying attention to the inner life rather than just to externals. Other people, however, will respond to this text in negative ways. We have experienced so much shame that we find it difficult to believe that Jesus is doing anything other than shaming these people. And we have experienced so much moralistic rejection that we find it difficult to believe that Jesus is understanding or sympathetic about the emotional pain in which pretense is rooted.

Encourage people to explore the reasons for their fears that Jesus is being shaming and moralistic. Make the point that strong, direct confrontation is not the same thing as abuse. Telling the truth may be painful, but no change can come unless our denial is confronted.

Question 3. One key root of pretense is the fear of rejection. Fear of rejection comes, of course, from experiences of rejection. It can be expressed in a variety of ways including perfectionism, workaholic and other addictive behaviors, low self-esteem and isolation.

Be aware that perfectionists may find this text to be fertile soil for their disease. Viewed through perfectionist lenses, this text says, "not only ought I to be perfect in my external behavior, I should be perfect in my motivations and attitudes as well." Nothing could be further from what Jesus is trying to say. The religious leaders to whom Jesus spoke were perfectionistic in the extreme about their external behavior. Jesus is not encouraging them to repeat this exercise with their inner life. He is confronting their denial in hopes that honesty will open them to the possibility of an entirely different way of being in the world, a way that is rooted in grace and freedom rather than in compulsion and shame.

Question 5. The lethal dose of pretense for faith is very low. Even a little can destroy our security and trust in God. It is a remarkable irony that people who are intellectually convinced that God knows everything would find themselves attempting to pretend with God. Pretense is driven, however, by very powerful forces.

Question 6. There is both a psychological and a spiritual link between honesty and healing. Psychologically, honesty is like opening the windows of a dark house to let in the light. In the dark, you will only stumble on the mess. With the windows open, the house can be cleaned. The mess might not be a pretty sight but you can do something about it. Spiritually, honesty is also important. At the heart of the Christian faith is the conviction that honesty makes possible a dramatic change in our relationship with God. Pretense distorts all spiritual realities. Honesty brings clarity and makes God's healing possible.

Question 8. It might help to distinguish between three kinds of fears: (a) Fears about the past. Sometimes we are attracted to pretense because we do not want to face guilt over decisions we have made in the past or because we are afraid that we have been so damaged by past events that we cannot be repaired. (b) Fears about the present. Sometimes we are attracted to pretense because we are afraid that we can't deal right now with the pain. We feel like we need to pretend just to make it through the day. (c) Fears about the future. Sometimes we are attracted to pretense because we are afraid that when people find out the truth about us they will abandon us or reject us. Whatever the reasons, fear leads to pretense and pretense leads to emotional and spiritual death. Jesus' invitation in this text is to live a life free from fear.

Study 2. Resisting Self-Righteousness: The Struggle to Acknowledge Our Needs. Luke 18:10-14.

Purpose: To encourage the acknowledgment of need.

Question 2. The central focus here is not on "confidence" as compared to "doubt" or on righteousness coming from within as compared to righteousness coming from God. Smugness about God-given righteousness is just as offensive as smugness about righteousness of any other kind. The point, rather, is that our self-understanding has implications for how we see other people. If our self-understanding is so distorted that we doubt our capacity for evil, then we will look down on lesser mortals. Unfortunately, forgetfulness about our capacity for evil is not limited to people with sociopathic personalities. We are all susceptible to self-righteousness, and it poisons many of our relationships.

Question 3. When we forget our capacity for evil, we are living in denial. Religious practices that reinforce this kind of denial may look spiritual, but they give no lasting peace because they cut us off from part of our self. Other common results of the pharisaic mentality are a toxic fear of being "found out" and perfectionism.

Question 4. The desire for purity can easily be distorted by comparing ourselves to other people. There will always be someone to whom we can compare ourselves favorably (for example, "Maybe I do have a drinking problem, but I'm not a lush like Fred"). As a result, comparisons tend to reinforce our denial about our own needs and our own failures.

Question 6. One of the central questions in interpreting this text is "What is it that Jesus approves about the tax collector?" People who are unable to be merciful with themselves are likely to think that Jesus is rewarding low self-esteem in the tax collector. From this perspective, the worse we feel about ourselves, the more likely God is to approve of us. But that is not at all what this text is about. This is a polemic against people who pretend they have no needs. Jesus' promise to needy people is that if we will face the truth about ourselves (humble ourselves) then we will experience God's blessing (be exalted).

Question 7. The differences are many. Here are three: (a) people with low self-esteem find it difficult to ask for help, while humble people are able to accept their own needs and ask for help; (b) people with low self-esteem are constantly comparing themselves unfavorably to others, while humble people do not have a comparative framework for self-evaluation; (c) people with low self-esteem find it difficult to accept either positive or negative feedback from others, while humble people are able to receive this kind of help.

Study 3. Resisting the Quick Fix: The Struggle to Persevere. Psalm 77:1-12.

Purpose: To encourage perseverance.

Question 4. Most people understand physical trauma. If you break a leg, people understand that it takes time to heal. If the trauma is emotional or spiritual, however, finding understanding is much more difficult. As a result, the social support we receive during recovery may be less than we expect—it may seem like people grow weary of our pain. And we get weary of it ourselves! When it seems like things have gone on and on and on and on—we just want it to be over. Sustaining hope over the long haul is a very challenging task.

Question 6. In all probability some members of your group will have experienced their community of faith as a very unsafe place to be a person in recovery. Stories of shame, rejection and abandonment are probable. You cannot undo the pain for people who have had bad experiences in the Christian community, but you can point them to the clear message of this text: pain is normal, recovery takes time, God doesn't give up on us because we are not better yet. Other members of your group may have experienced their community of faith as a helpful resource. Try to learn from them what qualities made the community a helpful resource.

Question 7. One of the most difficult parts of the recovery process is the struggle that goes on in our memories. This struggle is important because our memories compete with each other for positions of influence in our consciousness. The most powerful of our memories are the ones which will shape how we think and feel about the present and the future. The psalmist suggests that God offers us a set of memories which can compete effectively with our memories of abuse and neglect. The memory of God's works and mighty deeds can be more powerful than any other memory.

Study 4. Resisting Performance: The Struggle for Freedom and Grace. Micah 6:6-8; Ephesians 2:4-5, 8-9.

Purpose: To encourage the struggle for freedom and grace.

Question 2. People may think of a variety of examples of religious behaviors that can become compulsive. Some of these behaviors may be valuable and helpful if not distorted by our compulsivity. Prayer, for example, is a very practical and helpful religious practice. But if we turn prayer into an attempt to control reality or to coerce God into helping us get what we want, then we risk turning a helpful spiritual discipline into a compulsive, oppressive burden. Many other religious practices can become vehicles for our compulsivity: worship, evangelism, fasting. The key here is to see that God is not interested merely in the amount or frequency of our religious behaviors. God is interested in us.

Question 3. Performance-based spirituality is responsive to a variety of very basic human desires. (a) We have a desire for control. If I can perform some religious practice and I am confident that God is pleased, then I am a very powerful person. I can control God's mood! That's quite a powerful narcotic. Just as our unacknowledged desire for control can powerfully influence many other relationships, it can poison our relationship with God. (b) We have a desire for security. It is a seductively comforting thought that all I need to do is to repeat certain religious rituals or practices in a proscribed manner and my relationship with God will be complete. But intimacy in our relationship with God, like intimacy in any relationship, will not come merely from performances of any kind, no matter how well intentioned. (c) We have a desire for acceptance. If we have learned from an early age that acceptance is contingent upon our performance, then it is not difficult for us to project this kind of arrangement into our relationship with God. We perform for God. God accepts us. It may seem to some people like a workable arrangement. But it is an exchange that will eventually destroy any form of intimacy.

Question 4. The assumption is that God is an impossible task master who makes endless demands on us and who will withdraw his love or actively punish us if we do not meet up to his unrealistic expectations.

Question 5. The focus in the phrase "act justly and love mercy" is on our relationships with other people. The point is that God does not want us to be focused on performing but on developing loving relationships.

The focus in the phrase "walk humbly with your God" is on our relationship with God. It is a relationship which pictures us as his creatures or his children. This is not a picture of performing or proving ourselves, but of holding his hand and walking with him, recipients of his protection, care and guidance.

Question 6. In some parts of the Christian community, our relationship with God is understood primarily in terms of analogies to legal or commercial transactions. When these are the only analogies used to explain what the Christian faith is about, people often come to think of "getting saved" as a kind of "deal" that people make with God. If we pray the sinner's prayer, then God gives us salvation. Although the Bible does at times appeal to legal and commercial metaphors in trying to explain the nature of salvation, it is clear that the God of the Bible is a God who seeks much more than a "deal." God seeks to establish an intimate relationship with his people. God does not want merely to make a successful trade of "salvation" for "obedience" or "acceptance" for "religious performance." He has created us to be in relationship with himself and has gone to great lengths to make this possible.

Question 7. This text makes it clear that our relationship with God comes to us as a gift, given to us by God through Christ. It is a gift offered in love. Our part is to receive the gift of love that is offered.

Study 5. Resisting Judgmentalism: The Struggle for Compassion. Matthew 7:1-5; Galatians 6:1-2.

Purpose: To encourage the struggle for compassion.

Question 2. The appeal of judgmentalism is significant. If we know who the "bad" people are (them) and we know who the "good" people are (us), then judgmentalism can be very comforting. There is the comfort that comes from knowing that we have identified the problem, and it is not us. The more effort we put into identifying other people's failures, the more secure we may feel. There is also a kind of comfort that comes from judgmentalism because it is a powerful distraction from the emotional pain connected with our own sin and brokenness. If we can focus all of our attention on the "bad" people, then maybe we can postpone the painful realities which come when we focus on our own issues and problems.

Question 3. There are a long list of dangers with judgmentalism. (1) We are not qualified to judge others; we lack both the mercy and wisdom to judge well. (2) We are also not authorized to judge others; God has reserved this task for himself. (3) Judgmentalism has an addictive quality to it; many of us have found that we need to do more and more of it to get the same mood-altering effect. It is, therefore, a particular danger for anyone struggling with other addictive substances or processes. (4) Because it is an expression of our self-deceit and grandiosity, judgmentalism aggravates any existing dysfunctions. In particular it has a powerful eroding effect on intimate relationships. (5) Although it is not a conscious process, many of us have experienced that judgmentalism can result in a kind of self-rejection and self-loathing. Judgmentalism destroys our emotional immune system and leaves us vulnerable to self-destructive thoughts and feelings. What, we secretly wonder, would happen if we got what we deserved?

Question 4. Judgmentalism is rooted in denial about our own needs and is often accompanied by a grandiosity about our abilities to help others. Notice in the text from Matthew that Jesus is concerned about more than judgmental attitudes. He focuses on an offer of assistance ("Let me take the speck out of your eye"). Our judgmentalism is often masked as a kind of caring or helpful offer. Such "care," however sincere, will be destructive if it is rooted in a messianic self-concept or if it devalues the recipient.

Question 6. Some people find it helpful in resisting judgmentalism to distinguish between the "sin" and the "sinner." We reject the sin, but we love the sinner. While this is easy to say and might be helpful in some situations, it is usually not easy to put into practice. In the real world, the "sin" attaches very easily in our minds to the people involved, not merely to their behavior.

One of the central tasks in building Christian character is to increase our capacity to see past brokenness and evil in order to see the person whom God loves. Judgmentalism can't see that far. It sees only behaviors. Avoiding judgmentalism does not mean we should be passive when someone is involved with self-destructive behaviors. It is possible to actively care without caring compulsively or codependently. And it is possible to maintain healthy boundaries without abandoning people we care about. Not easy. But possible.

Question 7. Gentleness comes from a clear awareness of our own vulnerability to sin and failure. We restore with gentleness only when we are free from superiority and judgmentalism, when we know that we, too, may one day need to be restored.

Study 6. Resisting Legalism: The Struggle for Love. Luke 6:6-11.

Purpose: To encourage the struggle for love.

Question 2. Some people may be anxious about rule-breaking. Why not respect the tradition? Why make a big deal out of this? Didn't the Pharisees have good intentions? We feel anxious about breaking rules if they have provided us a sense of security and identity.

Other people will be relieved that Jesus makes such a clear statement that behavioral compliance is not an ultimate value in God's sight. It is good news that Jesus is far more concerned with our need for healing than with the keeping of religious rules.

Question 3. Jesus was deliberately achieving more than one purpose in this act. His concern for the man he healed was immediate and real. And so was his concern for the spiritual woundedness of the religious people and their leaders who had become so bound up by legalism that they had abandoned the law of love.

Question 4. Jesus' point is that rules and obligations necessarily serve some larger purpose. Sabbath rules were intended to serve a purpose bigger than the mere keeping of the Sabbath. The purpose of Sabbath-keeping is "to do good," "to save life." Jesus is appealing to an understanding of Sabbath keeping that had become lost by rigid enforcement of religious rules. The religious rulers and leaders valued rigid rule-keeping over the healing of this man.

Question 5. The religious leaders were very anxious when Jesus challenged their system with such power and authority. They had, after all, structured their whole reality around their rigid rules and exact standards of behavior. The rewards for following the rules are a sense of spiritual superiority and spiritual security. Rigid rules also allow us to feel in control. Jesus was calling the religious leaders (and is calling us!) to an entirely different way of life. It means seeing and grieving false ways. It means giving up rigid standards for comparing and measuring ourselves and others. It means developing a new personal identity. It means coming to a new understanding of God. All of this is very threatening. And our natural response when threatened is to get angry.

Question 6. This simple dramatic act by Jesus tells us a great deal about God. Much of it we may find difficult to believe, especially if we have come to see God through religious systems which are legalistic. This story tells us that God loves us, that he is aware of our need for healing, that he is responsive and compassionate and powerful to heal us, that he is interested in rules only if they protect us and give us life, that he will not abide by rules when they become destructive, that he wants to teach us the difference between rules that save life and rules that destroy life, and that he is a God who desires to give us life and to free us from all forms of bondage, including religious bondage.

For more information about Christian resources for people in recovery and subscription information for STEPS, *the newsletter of the National Association for Christian Recovery, we invite you to write to:*

The National Association for Christian Recovery
P.O. Box 11095
Whittier, California 90603

LIFE RECOVERY GUIDES FROM INTER-VARSITY PRESS
By Dale and Juanita Ryan

Recovery from Abuse. Does the nightmare of abuse ever end? After emotional, verbal and/or physical abuse how can you develop secure relationships? Recovery is difficult but possible. This guide will help you turn to God as you put the broken pieces of your life back together again. Six studies, 64 pages, 1158-3.

Recovery from Addictions. Addictions have always been part of the human predicament. Chemicals, food, people, sex, work, spending, gambling, religious practices and more can enslave us. This guide will help you find the wholeness and restoration that God offers to those who are struggling with addictions. Six studies, 64 pages, 1155-9.

Recovery from Bitterness. Sometimes forgiveness gets blocked, stuck, restrained and entangled. We find our hearts turning toward bitterness and revenge. Our inability to forgive can make us feel like spiritual failures. This guide will help us find the strength to change bitterness into forgiveness. Six studies, 64 pages, 1154-0.

Recovery from Codependency. The fear, anger and helplessness people feel when someone they love is addicted can lead to desperate attempts to take care of, or control, the loved one. Both the addicted person's behavior and the frenzied codependent behavior progress in a destructive downward spiral of denial and blame. This guide will help you to let go of over-responsibility and entrust the people you love to God. Six studies, 64 pages, 1156-7.

Recovery from Distorted Images of God. In a world of sin and hate it is difficult for us to understand who the God of love is. These distortions interfere with our ability to express our feelings to God and to trust him. This guide helps us to identify the distortions we have and to come to a new understanding of who God is. Six studies, 64 pages, 1152-4.

Recovery from Family Dysfunctions. Dysfunctional patterns of relating learned early in life affect all of our relationships. We trust God and others less than we wish. This guide offers healing from the pain of the past and acceptance into God's family. Six studies, 64 pages, 1151-6.

Recovery from Fear. Our fears revolve around certain basic issues—intimacy, risk, failure, loneliness, inadequacy and danger. But God offers us support, empowerment and courage to face fear in all areas of life. This guide will help us discover how God can enable us to face our fears. Six studies, 64 pages, 1160-5.

Recovery from Loss. Disappointment, unmet expectations, physical or emotional illness and death are all examples of losses that occur in our lives. Working through grief does not help us to forget what we have lost, but it does help us grow in understanding, compassion and courage in the midst of loss. This guide will show you how to receive the comfort God offers. Six studies, 64 pages, 1157-5.

Recovery from Shame. Shame is a social experience. Whatever its source, shame causes people to see themselves as unlovable, unworthy and irreparable. This guide will help you to reform your self-understanding in the light of God's unconditional acceptance. Six studies, 64 pages, 1153-2.

Recovery from Spiritual Abuse. Because of negative teaching we have received, many of us have learned that we have to earn our way with God. We have come to experience the Christian life as a burden—and a source of deep shame. Through these studies, we will discover that we can be healed of spiritual abuse and find freedom and grace in Christ. Six studies, 64 pages, 1159-1.